Old WORKSOP

by
David Ottewell

3630. TOWN HALL, WORKSOP.

Worksop Town Hall on Potter Street was built in 1851 in the Venetian Gothic style. The Dukes of Newcastle donated the clock that adorns the building's frontage, and their coat of arms is to be found above the front door. Over the years the building has been put to a number of uses, including serving as the town's corn market. At one time there were a series of slaughterhouses to its rear catering for traders on the adjacent market. For some years the county court and magistrates were also housed in the building. Between 1852 and 1902 the library of the Reading Society and Mechanics Institute, forerunner of the public library, had its headquarters in the town hall. It was also the venue for a number of other events including dances, plays, pantomimes and choir recitals.

© David Ottewell 2001
First published in the United Kingdom, 2001,
by Stenlake Publishing
Telephone / Fax: 01290 551122

ISBN 1 84033 157 7

FURTHER READING

The books listed below were used by the author during his research. None of them are available from Stenlake Publishing. Those interested in finding out more are advised to contact their local bookshop or reference library.

R. & I. Davies, *Worksop on Old Picture Postcards*, Reflections, 1995.
M. J. Jackson, *Worksop Yesterday*, Sissons and Sons.
M. J. Jackson, *Worksop in Times Past*, Countryside Publications, 1979.
J. Robb, *Turning Back The Pages in Old Worksop*, Nottinghamshire County Council, 1999.

There has been an inn called the French Horn on this site in Potter Street since the eighteenth century. The present building (featured here) dates from the first decade of the twentieth century and is much larger than the one it replaced. Its ornate facade reflects its prominent position opposite the town hall.

INTRODUCTION

The market town of Worksop is situated in the north of the county of Nottinghamshire, 26 miles from Nottingham and on the edge of the ancient Sherwood Forest. Its name is believed to derive from words meaning 'fortified hill'. The origins of Worksop are unclear, but a community most likely first developed in Saxon times when an area of raised sandstone in the valley of the River Ryton was chosen as a place to settle. It was a good strategic position, being both close to a supply of water and providing commanding views over the surrounding countryside.

By the time of the Domesday survey (1086) there was a large, established community in the area and the Norman newcomers built a castle to establish their presence. Further building took place in 1103 when the Augustinians built a monastery which became known as Radford Priory. This had a marked influence on those who lived nearby until it was shut down by Henry VIII in 1539. The monastic lands were given to the Earl of Shrewsbury who began to build a manor house in which to live. The 6th Earl demonstrated his wealth and influence by employing the most famous architect of the day, Robert Smythson, to design Worksop Manor.

Like many towns in rural England, Worksop remained a small, self-contained community with an economy based on agriculture and the associated industries of timber, milling and malting until the end of the eighteenth century. The opening of the Chesterfield Canal in 1777 helped to open up Worksop, providing an efficient means of transport for raw materials and finished goods in and out of the town.

The nineteenth century saw Worksop expand dramatically, with the population increasing fivefold. In 1849 the Manchester, Sheffield & Lincolnshire Railway Company took their line from Manchester to Grimsby through Worksop, providing another means of transporting goods to and from the town. Not to be outdone, the Midland Railway, wishing to expand northwards, built a line from Nottingham to join the MSL railway near Shireoaks. This was opened in 1875. The development of collieries in the area also helped accelerate the growth of

the town, starting with Shireoaks in 1859 and followed by Steetley, Whitwell, and finally Manton in 1907. As people came to Worksop in pursuit of work, so they created a demand for housing and other facilities such as schools, churches, chapels and shops.

The proximity of Worksop to the area of Sherwood Forest known as the Dukeries gave the town a noble air. As the nineteenth century progressed and people began to have more leisure time, so they were attracted to Worksop as a starting point for carriage tours of the Dukeries organised by local innkeepers. A number of members of the royal family used Worksop as a staging post as they arrived to visit local noble families on their country estates.

King George V granted Worksop its charter of incorporation in 1931. The town's coat of arms reflects its varied history and influences, featuring as it does a knight in armour and a Robin Hood type figure. It also includes a lion, an oak tree, five ducal coronets and a miner's pick and shovel.

WKP. 88.   CARLTON ROAD. WORKSOP.

Worksop's impressive war memorial was built in sight of the Priory Church on an island in the middle of a new road running between Watson Road and the church. It was unveiled by General Sir Horace Smith-Dorrien in June 1925. The road was christened Memorial Avenue and officially opened by King George V and Queen Mary in 1928.

The Priory Church of St Mary and St Cuthbert dates from the early part of the twelfth century when it was part of an Augustinian monastery. Much of the monastery was destroyed in the reign of Henry VIII. Until the building of St John's in 1868, the Priory Church was the only Anglican church in Worksop. Major restoration was carried out between 1845 and 1849 using plans drawn up by the Lincoln architect R. Nicholson. The twin towers are 90 feet high.

Potter Street, originally known as Pottergate, took its name from the potters who set up their stalls in this area. The building to the left is the Victorian town hall and the Market Place is just beyond it. The French Horn public house, featured on page 2, is situated just out of shot to the right, while in the foreground two rather grisly pigs' carcasses hang outside what was presumably a butcher's shop.

Worksop Market Place is to be found by the side of the town hall. For many years much of it was enclosed by buildings on the western side. The large shop to the right of this photograph belonged to David Winks & Sons, butchers. Potter Street can just be seen beyond branching off to the right with Hoosan Brothers, maltsters and grocers, on the corner.

Two large hotels – the Royal and the Lion (the latter has a shield-shaped badge like a pub sign hanging from it) – stood in Worksop Market Place, vying for business almost next door to each other. In this picture both are advertising garage accommodation in an attempt to attract the increasing numbers of passing motorists; both hotels were also starting points for carriage trips to the nearby Dukeries. The Royal Hotel closed in 1976 and was subsequently converted to retail premises. The ironmongery business on its near side, with an impressive array of tinware hanging up outside, belonged to Henry Philip Forrest.

Running down from the market area, Bridge Street was – and still is – the main shopping area of Worksop. It contained a number of public houses, one of which, the George Inn, can just be seen beyond the shop of F. Dunn & Sons, bootmakers, at no. 81. Only horse-drawn traffic is visible in this view, which dates from the beginning of the twentieth century.

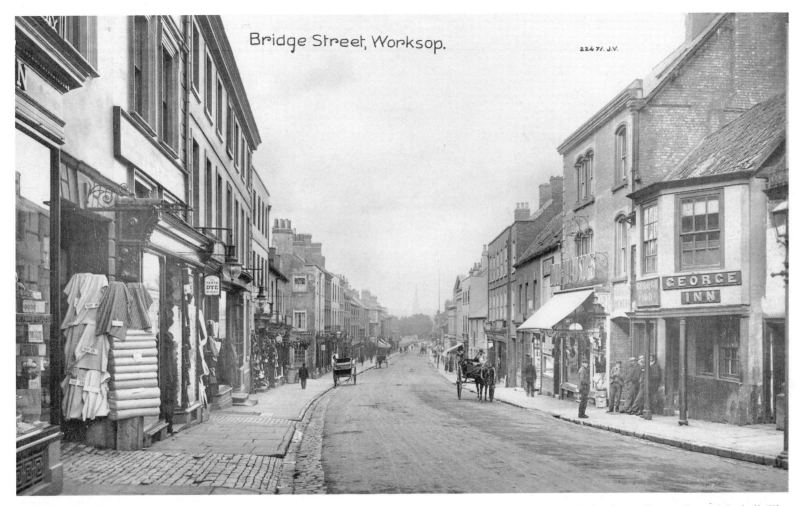

The ancient George Inn pictured just prior to closure in 1909. In the year previous to this the landlord is recorded as being George Ernest Mitchell. The George had experienced a long life as a coaching inn, but had also played a part in the life of the town in other ways. For many years magistrates held their monthly meeting in the Justices Room situated in the distinctive first floor bay. As the twentieth century dawned the inn's owners, the Worksop and Retford Brewery Company, decided to convert the premises to a shop and offices. On 20 January 1911 the *Worksop Guardian* commented: 'The disappearance of the Old George Inn will be regretted by many Worksop people.'

It was not unusual to see members of the military passing through Worksop during the First and Second World Wars, as the grounds of nearby large houses in the Dukeries were used for mustering and training troops prior to them being posted to the front. This group is riding along Bridge Street with the Golden Lion on the left at no. 57. Next door at no. 55 are the premises of Henry Winfrow, tobacconist, with the Savings Bank on the far side of the pub. The Worksop Yeomanry left the town for France on 10 August 1914.

The Old Ship (left) is claimed to be the oldest pub in Worksop. Its name is said to derive from a series of wooden beams in the inn which were salvaged from ships that were broken up after the battle of Trafalgar.

94-5. Bridge St. Worksop. J.S.&S.

A comparison of this picture with the one on the front cover reveals that considerable changes have occurred in the intervening fifteen to twenty years. Most notable is that all the road transport is now motorised. The appearance of the building on the corner of Castle Street has been transformed by the addition of a mock Tudor facade, a feature which it retains to this day.

Bridge Street in the 1950s. The Maypole Dairy Company's shop stood at no. 68. At one time this company had branches in most of the local towns.

The bottom of Bridge Street close to its junction with Newcastle Avenue. The impressive building seen in profile on the left was built in the early years of the twentieth century and was initially known as the Arcade. When completed it comprised two rows of shops and a central linking section and was called Central Buildings.

Bridge Street, Worksop.

Barclays Bank, on the corner of Bridge Street and Newcastle Avenue, was built in the gap visible at the left of the previous picture (once the site of the cattle market). The roof of the arcade of shops extending from the bank is topped by a series of pointed spires, some of which today are sadly no longer *in situ*.

Looking down an unusually empty Newcastle Avenue. This half of Central Buildings (round the corner from and at right angles to the portion seen on page 15) once accommodated Heywood's shoe shop, B. Wright ('The One Price Tailor'), Haywood's confectioners and A. C. Ilett, saddler. Beyond the shops, obscured by the telegraph pole, is the Electric Theatre. In the days of silent films this was the only one of Worksop's four cinemas to provide accompaniment on an organ. Later it was the first cinema to introduce talkies to the town. Walking up the road towards the camera are a trio of postmen. The building just beyond the Electric Theatre was the new post office, which opened in 1910 to replace the old one on Potter Street.

A postcard featuring Ezra Taylor's photographic shop at no. 6 Bridge Place (right foreground). Taylor took hundreds of photographs of Worksop and the surrounding area and sold substantial numbers of copies in the form of postcards. This one was sent by one of Mr Taylor's family who wrote on the back: 'Look at this postcard and you will see me and Lizzie looking in the shop window. Lizzie is in black me with light coat on.' The Congregational Church, next to Taylor's shop, was built in 1876.

For a long time Victoria Square was known as Common End. This view shows the north side of the square with Gateford Road to the left and Carlton Road to the right. The building in the centre was constructed in the 1870s. The shop to the right, on the corner of Carlton Road, was a sub post office run for many years by the Pennington family.

The premises of Castle & Sons, carriage and harness manufacturers, on the western side of Victoria Square, form the backdrop to William Sumner's photograph of the 1908 Empire Day celebrations. Not many years later the site was redeveloped and the Victoria Palace Theatre was built here (see overleaf).

GATEFORD ROAD, WORKSOP.

The Victoria Palace Theatre opened on 2 November 1914 with space for an audience of 730. They could pay 3*d*., 4*d*., or 6*d*. to watch silent films in the stalls, or splash out 9*d*. to really treat themselves and sit in the balcony. Talkies began to be shown in October 1931, by which time the seating capacity had been reduced to 612. A name-change occurred in 1940 when the cinema reopened as the Savoy, enjoying a further twenty years of life before finally closing in January 1960.

ST. JOHN'S CHURCH, WORKSOP

As a result of Worksop's expansion in the mid-nineteenth century, a second Anglican church was required in the town. In 1867 a separate parish was formed and plans were put in place to build St John's, which opened the following year. It was built in the Early English style, and the embattled tower with broach spire was a particular feature. This view is interesting because the Marquis of Waterford Inn (the white building just to the right of the tower) and the houses on Sandy Lane have all been demolished in recent years.

The spire of St John's helps to locate this picture of Ashley House on Gateford Road. At one time the house belonged to Mordecai Binney, a local tanner. In the 1850s it was sold to Humphrey Parry who turned it into a private boys' school, part of which was for boarders. The school transferred to 'Oakholme', off Carlton Road, in 1930.

The Travellers Rest – quite a common local pub name – was also on Gateford Road, and here the landlord and his family pose for the camera. In 1905 the licence-holder was Alfred Edward Reed.

Carlton Road, Worksop.

Carlton Road as it leaves the north-east side of Victoria Square. The gents' toilets appear to be a new feature, and aren't present in the picture on page 18. There were two garages in this first short section of Carlton Road, one advertising Standard cars, the other Fords, reflecting the increase in motor transport from the 1920s onwards.

Carlton Road was at the wealthier end of Worksop and consisted mainly of better quality housing predominantly constructed in the second half of the nineteenth century. The building on the left is the Station Hotel, built prior to 1873 to cater for both tourists and commercial travellers arriving in the town by rail. In spite of the passing horse and cart, which would have been a familiar sight in Edwardian times when this picture was taken, the hotel is advertising a motor garage as part of its facilities. It had perhaps moved with the times, converting its stables to cater for the new form of horsepower.

In 1849 the Manchester, Sheffield and Lincolnshire Railway Company built a line through Worksop and employed architects Weightman and Hadfield to design a station in the town for them. They were instructed that it should be quite ornate, as it would be catering for a large number of passengers, many of whom would be attracted to the area by the Dukeries. Local company James Drabble of Carlton in Lindrick built the station at a cost of £7,850, using white Steetley stone. It opened on 7 July 1849. In 1875 the Midland Railway Company also began using Worksop station, with trains running to Kings Cross in the south and Sheffield and Manchester in the north. The company changed its name to the Great Central Railway Company in 1897, and at the same time improved the station with extensions, including waiting areas and refreshment rooms, longer platforms and a canopy.

Watson Road, which was developed between 1870 and 1900, was named after the chief landowner in the area, Sir Henry Watson, who lived at Park Cottage. Sir Henry acted as a benefactor to a number of local causes including donating the land on which the Victoria Hospital was built. The public library was built in Watson Road in 1902, and remained there until it was transferred to its present site on Memorial Avenue.

In 1897 the townspeople of Worksop looked for an appropriate way to celebrate the Diamond Jubilee of the reign of Queen Victoria. The decision was made to build a hospital in the town. Up until this time if people fell ill they either went to the dispensary on Potter Street, or in extreme cases had to make the uncomfortable journey to Sheffield for treatment. Donations were made and fund-raising events held and on 24 May 1900 the Victoria Hospital was opened on Watson Road, initially with five beds. Each year there was a Hospital Day Procession to raise money for the hospital. The Coronation of George V inspired the locals to extend the hospital and on 7 November 1912 the Duchess of Portland opened a new Coronation wing, while Sir John Robinson of Worksop Manor opened a Children's wing. Other extensions were added in 1925. The hospital was demolished in June 1996.

2515. The Hospital, Worksop

A rural view of the Priory Church photographed from the north. To its right is the Abbey School for girls, the buildings of which still stand on Priorswell Road. In Edwardian times the school could accommodate 200 girls, and the headmistress was Miss Sarah Ann Smith. The Abbey School for boys was close by on Potter Street.

A snowy view of Worksop, with the Abbey Tea Warehouse (proprietor John Saxton) at 9–13 Cheapside to the left. A huge sign advertises 'Delicious Butters, Fresh and Pure' – these would have been cut from the block to individual requirements. The 'Finest Teas, Coffees and Sugars' would again have been purchased loose at this time. Across the road to the right is a cycle shop, a familiar sight in the early years of the twentieth century when cycling was hugely popular.

Lowtown Street was one of the roads running off Cheapside. The crowd of children are gathered outside the Fox Inn. There had been a public house situated here since at least 1862 and in 1912 the landlord was listed as John Lees.

Park Street looking towards the market area. The Blue Bell Inn was owned by the Worksop and Retford Brewery Company, whose head office was in the town. Between 1895 and 1915 Mrs Elizabeth Trafford was the licensee. This was a popular pub name in Worksop, and there were also Blue Bell Inns on West Street and Norfolk Street. The last landlord listed for the pub is Ernest Ellis in 1933.

Park Street looking from the opposite direction to the previous picture (the sign on the left, reading 'H. Wright & Son, Painters & Paperhangers', is visible in both views). All the buildings on the left-hand side remain today, although H. Wright's premises is now a house.

The School, St Mary's Church, Worksop.

The Presbytery, St Mary's Church, Worksop.

Park Street once led to Worksop Manor park. At one time the manor belonged to the Duke of Norfolk, whose family were Roman Catholics. St Mary's Catholic Church was built on Park Street in 1840, and its associated school dated from the same period.

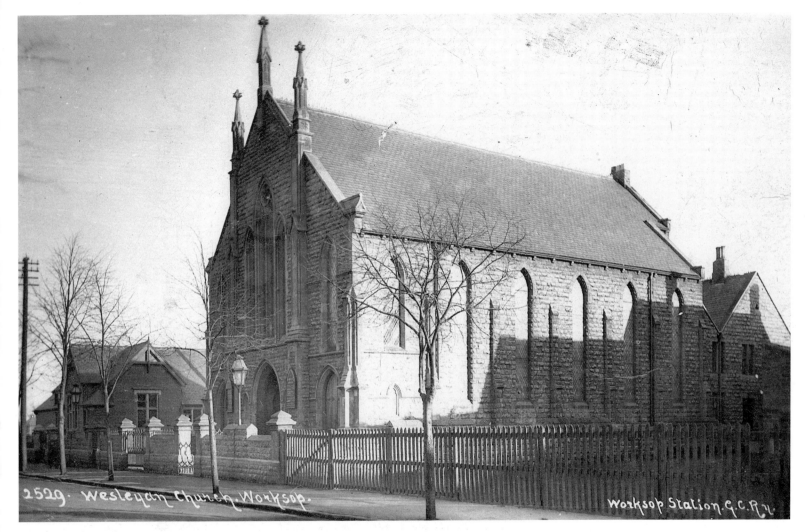

2529. Wesleyan Church. Worksop.

Worksop Station. G.C.R.Y.

Different religions played an important part in the life of Worksop. John Wesley visited the town on 29 July 1780, when he preached on Lead Hill, although it was over 20 years before the Wesleyans had a home to be proud of in Worksop. The Wesleyan church, with schoolroom and vestry, opened in 1803 and could accommodate 764 worshippers. It was seriously damaged by fire in June 1969, necessitating a complete rebuild.

Below: Royal visits were occasions to be prized. This picture shows part of the crowd awaiting the arrival of King Edward VII in December 1905. The onlookers are massed at the corner of the Market Place with the side of the town hall to the right and the top of Potter Street to the left. Special stands had to be erected to give a good view of the royal party as they passed by in a horse-drawn carriage. Photographers (Chadwick & Allen of Hull in this case) often took extensive views of crowds in the hope of selling large numbers of postcards, in local shops, to people who wanted a souvenir of themselves attending a special event.

ROYAL VISIT TO WORKSOP DEC. 11ᵗʰ 1905

Flags and bunting adorned the route that the royal party travelled. These decorations were at the top end of Bridge Street close to the George Inn.

Royal Visit to Worksop.   Dec. 11th, 1905.—No. 4.

King George V and Queen Mary passing through Worksop on 30 November 1912. During their visit to Nottinghamshire they stayed with the Duke and Duchess of Portland at Welbeck Abbey. The party arrived and departed from the station and local crowds took advantage of the opportunity to see their monarch.

The generous hospitality offered by the Duke and Duchess of Portland at Welbeck Abbey and the Savile Family at Rufford Abbey in the Dukeries meant the frequent presence of members of the royal family in Nottinghamshire. Here the Prince of Wales has been photographed by Ezra Taylor of Bridge Place after reviewing the local cadet force. The date is believed to be July 1923.

The Brewery Offices, Worksop.

The Worksop and Retford Brewery Company was formed in 1881 with the amalgamation of Smith and Nephew and the Priorwell Brewery Company. Brewing was concentrated in the Priorwell Road works where extensive expansion took place. The buildings were demolished in 1962.

An aerial view said to have been taken from the top of the electricity works chimney. This area was known as Radford, taking its name from the 'red ford', a crossing point on the River Ryton. The Boundary Inn on Cheapside marked the dividing line between Radford and Worksop, which for many years were two distinct settlements. The Priory Church lies on the far side of the road, while nearer the camera is the Priory Mill, situated on the Canch (a dam made on the River Ryton). Most of the open ground has long since disappeared under pressure for much-needed housing.

The Canch. Worksop.

Priory Mill took its name from the neighbouring church, the twin towers of which can just be seen in the background of this picture. The Canch was the name of the dam that was used to harness the water's powers to drive the mill machinery, although eventually the power source was changed from water to steam. Originally the building was used as a corn mill for Worksop Priory, but when the demand for milling declined the mill's owner, the Duke of Newcastle, rented it out. William Bramer became a tenant. He was a chair-maker and worker in wood whose previous premises had burnt down. Unfortunately for him a fire broke out at Priory Mill in 1912 and the building was destroyed.

The firm of John Shaw Ltd. was founded in Sheffield in 1820 and initially manufactured wire products such as arches, baskets, sieves and screens. Later they also produced wrought-iron wares such as fences and gates, and in 1860 started making wire ropes, challenging manufacturers of hemp ropes and chains. The company prospered and by the 1870s were exporting to South Africa, New Zealand and Australia. When their Sheffield factory was destroyed in an air raid on 12 December 1940 they opened this new factory in Worksop.

There were a variety of sporting groups in Worksop, with football and cricket clubs fielding a number of teams in the appropriate seasons. Worksop Town FC has reached the FA Cup third round on four occasions. The last was in 1955–6 when they lost 1–0 to Swindon Town. Their most famous fixture was in the 1922–3 season when they met Tottenham Hotspur in the third round at White Hart Lane. They held Spurs to a goal-less draw in front of a crowd of 23,929. Unfortunately they lost the replay 9–0. There was also a golf course at Carlton in Lindrick, and a tennis club, members of which are pictured here.

This photograph, taken by the prolific Ezra Taylor, shows a Ladies' Day gathering at the cricket club and bowling green. The Worksop area has been a centre for a number of famous sportsmen over the years. The many times world snooker champion and first player to officially compile a 147 break, Joe Davies, was born at Whitwell while cyclist Tommy Simpson, who tragically died during the 1967 Tour de France, lived at Harworth. Today Worksop-born Lee Westwood is making a name for himself in the world of golf.

They were a hardy lot in Worksop in the early years of the last century. Here the photographer William Sumner, based at 49 Bridge Street, has captured the crowd at the opening of the outdoor swimming baths. The twin towers of the Priory Church stand in the background.

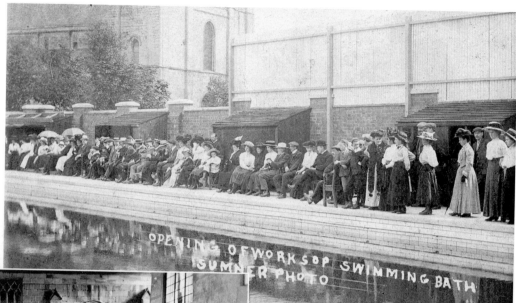

Local religious groups, especially the Methodists, put on yearly events such as bazaars to raise money for good causes. Often the venue was the town hall. This one was designated 'Old Worksop' and took place in 1912. It included a very lifelike model of the Priory Gatehouse and market cross, along with other scenes from around the town.

Newcastle Avenue was chosen by Sir John and Lady Anne Robinson of Worksop Manor as an appropriate site for the building of a third Anglican church in Worksop. They were concerned about the distance of the two established churches from their home, and the new site was nearer. Architects Austen and Paley were employed to design the church, and its foundation stone was laid by the Robinson family in 1911. The design included a bell tower, but no bells were fitted until June 1977 when eight were purchased from the burnt-out church of All Saints, Pitsmoor, Sheffield. St Ann's was consecrated by Sir Edwyn Hoskyns, Bishop of Southwell, on 24 November 1912. The war memorial outside St Ann's is a later addition but was erected prior to the one featured on page 4.

St Anne's Memorial and Newcastle Avenue, Worksop.

Sparken Hill formed the main southerly route into Worksop. When this postcard was sent in 1913 the road had a very rural outlook with only a pair of horse-drawn vehicles occupying the thoroughfare. Today there are buildings on both sides of the road as one descends into Worksop.

SPARKEN HILL, WORKSOP (4)   223811. J.V.

Rose Cottage standing in splendid isolation close to the summit of Sparken Hill. Even today, with the demand for building land, it still has few neighbours. In the past residents of the cottage looked for ways to supplement their income, and at one time bags of sand, acquired from the outcrop behind the building, were sold to passers-by. In this 1940s' picture the cottage has a sign advertising Apollo table waters for sale.

The original Worksop Manor was Elizabethan, and was designed by the famous architect Robert Smythson for the 6th Earl of Shrewsbury. It was an extremely high-status home, and was visited by Mary, Queen of Scots, James I and Charles I. A tragic fire saw it burn down in 1761. Following this, work on a new house was undertaken by the then owner, the Duke of Norfolk, but was never completed, and in 1840 ownership passed to the Duke of Newcastle whose family home was Clumber House. He demolished much of the pre-1840 structure. From 1890 the manor became the family home of Sir John and Lady Anne Robinson.

A.239-541. Castle Farm, Worksop. Copyright. Scrivens

When the 9th Duke of Norfolk inherited Worksop Manor in 1732, he and his wife set about a scheme of improvements. One of the Duchesses pet projects was the design of a new range of buildings in the form of a quadrangle, containing offices, a dairy and – most importantly – a private sitting room where she could keep her extensive collection of horticultural books. Edwin Eddison, writing in his 1840 *History of Worksop*, praised the Worksop Manor estate and described the Castle Farm thus: 'Its Gothic front, embattled parapet and castle like appearance added greatly to the effect of the scene.'

A.239-542. Castle Farm, Worksop. Copyright. Scrivens

Worksop College was originally known as St Cuthbert's School and was one of a group of Church of England schools founded by Canon Nathaniel Woodward in the second half of the nineteenth century. It was built on a site donated by the 8th Duke of Newcastle. The buildings were designed by R. H. Carpenter, and when the school opened in 1895 it initially had four masters and 25 boys. It proved extremely popular and pupil numbers rose to 100 within a year, prompting further building work.

The library, Worksop College.